A sweet friendship refreshes the soul.

– Proverbs 27:9

Contents

Poetry

From The Manse Window

A Year In Nature

Illustrations by Manon Gandiolle and Mandy Dixon.

A Special Guest

A special guest is on her way –
She visits every year.
She packs her travel bag with smiles,
Sweet songs of hope and cheer.

She brings the gift of longer days,
A beautiful bouquet
Of tulips, as a thank-you for
Inviting her to stay.

She's welcomed with the rousing sound
Of trumpet fanfare when
The daffodils announce her grand
Arrival once again.

She starts her joyful season with
The promise of rebirth,
Sprinkles April showers, breathes
New life into the earth.

She keeps a crown of daisies as
A souvenir, too,
Then says goodbye in June before
The summer sun is due.

Michelle Illing

A Mother's Love

In the midst of caring families is the glue that holds them fast,
A source of inspiration, unconditional love that lasts.
A hub round which the family stays, still anchored yet spread wide,
A free and flowing, wandering sea, held gently by the tide.
A mother is this centre around which her children grow,
She tends and waters carefully the seeds of life she sows.
She is that shining pathway that can lead us through dark nights.
A mother's love is endless and her guiding light is bright.

Linda Brown

Transcendence

In the grey-blue of the day
And almost Easter
There in the evening
The four swans lighting the loch.

Like things struck white –
The shore, the hills, the sky
All dulled and somehow under them.

Like angels birthed
In the still becoming of the year,
The un-resurrected grey.

I stand at the window watching,
See the grace of my own hands
Until they lift in rough graces
And strengthen into the wind –

Bringing a birthing, a new beginning
So afterwards the land remembers them
Is left still shining.

Kenneth Steven

Sunday Rider

Bells ring as we set off together –
Somehow, they've convinced me to come.
"Don't be silly; of course you'll remember.
It's easy and good healthy fun!"

The skills we so easily mastered
When we were all young and carefree,
Feel rusty now I'm getting older
With aches in my hips, back and knees.

Determined, I clip on my helmet
And gamely push off from the kerb.
I wobble my way round a storm drain,
Steeling what's left of my nerve.

The burn in my thighs is terrific
On the hill, as I puff to the top;
The freewheeling down makes it worth it –
Oh, my gosh! How on earth do I stop?

At last, lunch is on the horizon,
The Cricketer's Arms is in sight.
I've still got to face the ride back, though.
No doubt I shall sleep well tonight.

Laura Tapper

Treasured Tales

The rabbits on the roundabout
Are nibbling at the grass.
I smile and sigh as I drive by,
Enchanted as I pass.
Their pompom tails delight me
As they graze there without care,
And secretly I wish that I could
Stay and stand and stare.
My childhood treat was bedtime tales
Of rabbits you may know,
So let me sigh as I pass by
Miss Potter's quaint tableau.

Judy Jarvie

from the Manse Window

A Little Bit of Everything

NEAR the popular Spanish Steps in Rome is All Saints' Anglican Church.

It was the venue for a Baroque ensemble playing "The Four Seasons" by Antonio Vivaldi a few years ago.

My wife and I were in the city on holiday and had the pleasure of attending an evening of top-notch classical music in a beautiful venue.

A Baroque ensemble is smaller than a full orchestra. I think there were just nine musicians that evening but, my, how they could play!

The opening lines of "Spring" are quite up-tempo, and we felt a little like giggling as the row of formally dressed, slightly demure players suddenly seemed to burst into vigorous life.

The ones with longer hair might almost have been "headbanging" at a rock concert!

Particularly impressive was the young violin virtuoso, who played for almost an hour from memory without a single note of music in

front of him. Wonderful stuff!

"The Four Seasons" is an interesting piece of music – actually four violin concertos, one for each season.

They're believed to have been composed by Vivaldi around 1720, when he was Chapel Court Master in Mantua. While he wrote a vast amount of music during his career, including some 50 operas, this is probably his best-known work.

What made it innovative was its descriptive quality; how the composer painted various scenes from the year in the music.

We can listen for representations of flowing streams, buzzing flies, storms, a shepherd and his (barking) dog, a hunting party, the fireside in winter and even a bit of drunken partying!

A little bit of everything, one might say, or we could simply call it what it is: a masterpiece.

Now, while I love music, as a minister I actually have a much greater love for scripture.

As I was musing on this, I ▶

iStock.

By Rev. Andrew Watson.

All Saints' Anglican Church, Rome.

thought on how the New Testament Gospels have an intriguing selection – a little bit of everything – as they describe that fateful Passover week in Jerusalem.

In our part of the world, we sometimes say the weather gives us all four seasons in one day!

Observe with me how all four seasons are reflected in the developing drama of what would become the first Easter.

Spring dawns with golden daffodils and promise. New life and hope feel possible again. Picture Christ riding into Jerusalem on Palm Sunday, crowds cheering and waving branches.

They'd heard so much about him. The sick healed, the hungry fed, and an inspiring message of new spiritual beginnings with God as a loving, forgiving father.

Could this unorthodox teacher from Galilee possibly be the good king they'd been promised and had waited for?

The promise seemed to intensify, like the perennials flowering in the garden, as Jesus barred corrupt dealers from the temple, but welcomed little children and the poor who were seeking redemption.

God's house seemed to be blossoming!

Summer approaches and we dream of sandy beaches and sunshine, but the increased heat can fuel tension on the streets even as the skies threaten thunder.

Those captivated by tradition and control oppose the new preacher, rumbling discontent, demanding credentials and spreading slander.

He responds with thinly disguised parables, suggesting some of them are unfruitful stewards and are actually ripe for God's judgement.

Every day there is healing and revelation, but also controversy.

Autumn is perhaps one of the most beautiful seasons, and yet it is laced with tragedy.

The leaves turn red and gold, but then they fall. We witness majestic sunsets, but the days grow short and we zip our coats against the growing chill.

Jesus is betrayed by a close associate. Another close friend denies even knowing him.

Enemies carry through an appalling injustice to have this good and kind man arrested and condemned.

The Lord is "overwhelmed with sorrow" as the night closes in, darker than ever.

And yet he also shares his bread with his friends at the Last Supper, kneels like a servant to wash their dusty feet, and in memorable words assures a safe, eternal dwelling in the father's heavenly house to all who will trust and obey.

Something dreadful and sinister is moving in the shadows, but he is still demonstrating achingly beautiful love.

Never was divinity so profoundly vulnerable. The colours have grown deep and intense.

Suddenly it is winter and like a horror story the earth is lashed with icy rain.

People run for shelter, but for him there is none. Abandoned and alone, he accepts the worst abuse this jealous world can give.

Despised and rejected, beaten and tortured, he is hoisted on a cross to die.

The sky becomes unnaturally dark at midday, as though creation itself were ashamed.

From his agony, he is heard to utter some final words of grace, asking his mother and disciples to look after each other, incredibly praying, "Father, forgive them", and, at last, "It is finished!"

With that, he is dead.

The trees are bare, the land frozen and hard. Nicodemus and Joseph hurriedly put the body in a borrowed tomb.

It's over; the tragedy is complete. The seasons have run their course, catching our hearts in their colour and drama.

A little bit of everything – but is this where it ends? Is the cemetery the inevitable cold finale for us all?

Well, the Gospels are not quite finished. Without exception the witnesses testify to what they saw on that first day of the new week.

The tomb miraculously opened, and Jesus, risen and alive, calling us by name, showing us in his hands and side the wounds of love, commissioning us to share this wonderful news of hope with the world.

We notice crocuses and snowdrops where before there were none. Perhaps a new spring is possible?

Perhaps the real music has just begun! ■

A Year In Nature:

Spring

Fascinating facts about
Rabbits

■ If a rabbit gets excited, you might be lucky enough to catch it having a binky – the word used for the hop and twist they perform when they're happy! It's a sure sign of a happy rabbit.

■ Rabbits' eyes – placed on the side of their heads – give them an almost 360 degree field of vision. They can even see up above their heads, as well as behind them. The only blind spot they have is a small area just in front of their nose.

■ Rabbits can sleep with their eyes open. Even if they're fast asleep, light still gets in and gives their brain the signal to wake up if danger approaches. When they're awake, they only blink 10 to 12 times an hour.

■ A baby rabbit – a kit – only needs to feed once every 24 hours. Amazingly, they receive enough milk from their mum to keep them going, feeding only for 5 to 10 minutes. At just three weeks old they're on to solid foods.

■ Unlike humans or cats and dogs, rabbit teeth never stop growing. They're kept in check by constantly grazing on abrasive foods. Hay is great for this, which is why it makes up about 80-90% of pet rabbit diets.

Side By Side

Holding hands and giggling,
Lying side by side
On a threadbare faded carpet
In a sunbeam, six feet wide.

Turning heads and kissing,
In love and starry-eyed,
Imagining our pillows
For ever side by side.

Looking up and laughing –
Know what I've just realised?
They've taken all the lightbulbs;
I can't believe my eyes.

Holding hands and listening;
What's that noise outside?
I think it's them already –
The removal van's arrived!

Jumping up and running down
To welcome them inside;
Let's make this house into a home –
Get the front door open wide.

Kathryn Sennen

Worth Every Penny

A therapist works on our high street
With curlers, sharp scissors and spray.
Her invaluable care
Is reliably there
With a smile, though she works hard all day.

Customers might start at the basin,
Where a massage releases their stress.
It flows down the plug,
Washed away with the suds
While she listens – it's what she does best.

At the mirror she trims and reshapes them
As they chat about family and health,
Or with colour applied,
Cup of tea by their side,
They relax with some time to themselves.

Then they're blow-dried and styled to perfection
As, with skill, she creates their new "do".
They arrive in distress,
Or a bit of a mess,
But they wave goodbye feeling brand new.

Laura Tapper

A Walk In May

I fancied a walk in the country
And I'd found a new path to explore.
Off I went, with my stick and a rucksack
That held coffee and biscuits galore.

The path took a gentle slope upwards –
Tall nettles and brambles were growing;
The track became stony and narrow –
I'll admit, it was rather hard going.

But, oh, it was so worth the effort!
The path then meandered for miles;
I wandered through wildflower meadows,
Climbed over some quaint little stiles.

There was nothing to hear but the birdsong.
It was warm, and the sky blue and clear.
I saw sparrows and blackbirds and finches,
Some scampering squirrels, and deer.

And then the path wound even higher
Through trees that impeded the view.
I gasped as I walked through the woodland –
Spring flowers formed a carpet of blue.

And just when I thought it was perfect –
A splendour you just could not beat –
I emerged from the woods and discovered
A viewpoint, complete with a seat!

So here I sit, utterly spellbound,
So glad I set out to explore . . .
That view, and my coffee and biscuits –
I quite simply could not ask for more!

Emma Canning

A Clover Lawn

There are plants not allowed in some gardens,
In borders, on lawns, weeded out;
And clover is one,
Much derided by some,
That quite lately I've heard all about.

White, pink and purple its colours,
It is beautiful, fragrant and sweet;
It gives cover in drought,
It will survive without doubt,
While the grass on a lawn can't compete.

Your lawn will stay green all the summer
With little or no water lost;
With no mowing to do,
And no lawn feeding, too;
Just think how you'll save on the cost.

All the wildlife will thank you for clover,
But the bees you will find love it most;
It's also a treat
To walk on with bare feet,
And their honey is scrumptious on toast!

Dawn Lawrence

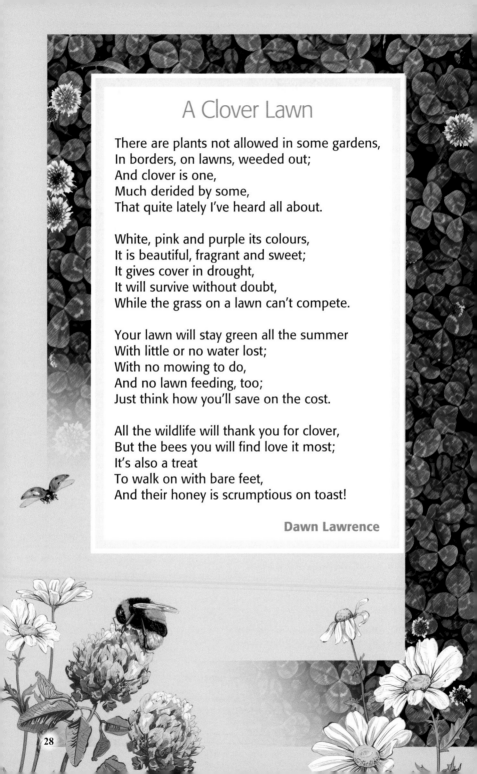

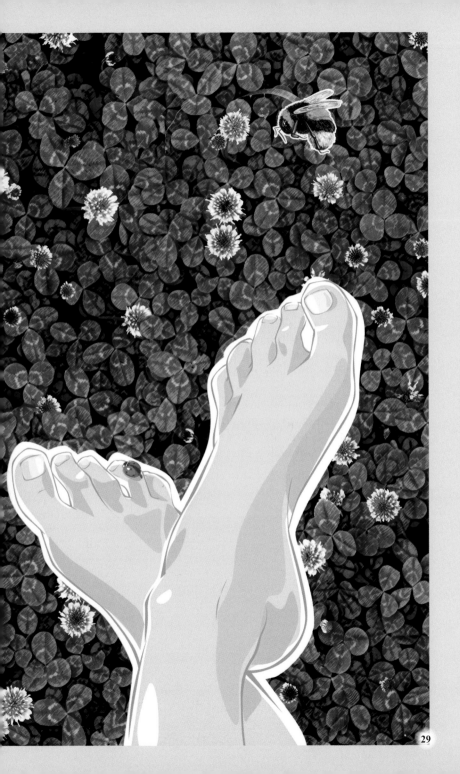

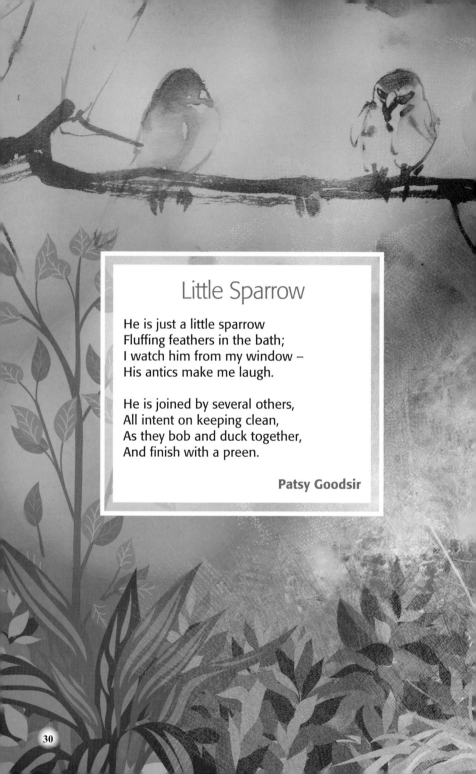

Little Sparrow

He is just a little sparrow
Fluffing feathers in the bath;
I watch him from my window –
His antics make me laugh.

He is joined by several others,
All intent on keeping clean,
As they bob and duck together,
And finish with a preen.

Patsy Goodsir

Bookmarks

I really must buy some new bookmarks –
I have none at all to be found!
I'm relying on various items
That I've simply had lying around . . .

I can't bear to bend a page corner
So I'm using whatever's to hand:
A small scrap of paper, a ribbon,
Or even an elastic band!

Today I looked though some old favourites,
Where I'd hurriedly, once, marked a place,
And the items I found in their pages
Brought such a big smile to my face!

A receipt from a meal with my daughter,
A programme I'd kept from a play,
A ticket for train rides to London
(Gosh, that was a wonderful day!)

A leaflet of local attractions
From a long-ago summer weekend,
And a tag with a very sweet message
From a gift that was sent by a friend . . .

It's a little untidy, I grant you,
But I shan't buy new bookmarks yet . . .
I've decided I like my old system –
What lovely reminders I get!

Emma Canning

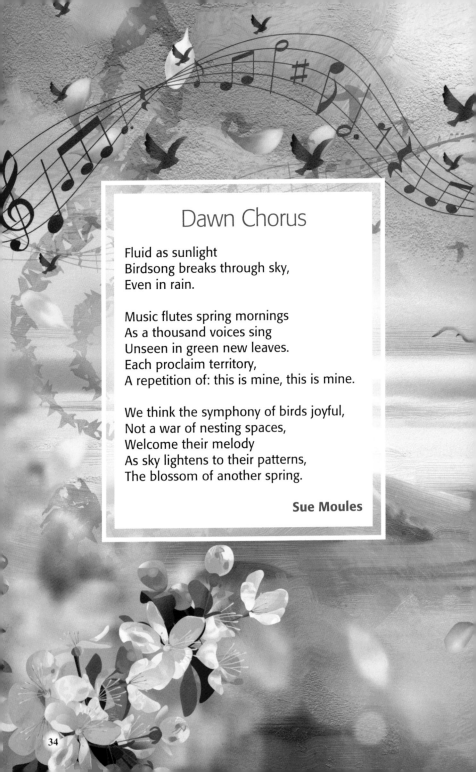

Dawn Chorus

Fluid as sunlight
Birdsong breaks through sky,
Even in rain.

Music flutes spring mornings
As a thousand voices sing
Unseen in green new leaves.
Each proclaim territory,
A repetition of: this is mine, this is mine.

We think the symphony of birds joyful,
Not a war of nesting spaces,
Welcome their melody
As sky lightens to their patterns,
The blossom of another spring.

Sue Moules

Time To Stand And Stare

MOST of us have our favourite season, but if there is one that is loved by pretty well everyone, then it has to be spring.

The sight of the first snowdrops, daffodils, primroses and pussy willows doesn't just lift the spirits, it also brings clear reassurance that the days are definitely getting longer and the worst of the weather is over.

And even if the spring days do insist upon bringing a few showers with them, at least they are interspersed with increasingly blue skies and sunshine.

I'm happy to say that there is one spring treat in which we may indulge even before winter has left us, for this is the time of year when we can really start looking at all those tempting new garden catalogues and making plans.

Whether we have a plot of our own, access to a community garden or just a tiny balcony, the chance to daydream over pictures of flowers and vegetables is a most effective way to raise spirits on a dark wet evening.

Even if we have no outdoor space at all, there's almost certainly a window-sill on which we could grow a few crisp salad leaves or a sweet-smelling hyacinth to dispel any lingering winter blues.

When it comes to finding space, my friend Bobbie has the opposite dilemma, for her garden is large and had been neglected for a long time before she moved in two years ago.

Despite being a novice gardener, she's not been deterred from doing her best to make it look as good as she can, and is always keen to receive tips from those who have already learned from their own mistakes!

It was a rather chill afternoon when I went to visit her. I found her studying photos that she'd taken the year before.

"It's an idea I was given last summer," she explained.

"Someone suggested that if I took lots of photographs of the garden throughout the ▶

iStock.

By Maggie Ingall.

Growing plants can dispel lingering winter blues.

year, then it would remind me of what worked well and what didn't.

"So that's what I did, and now I'm going through them all to help me plan my spring planting."

It sounded rather a good idea to me.

"Are you finding them helpful?" I asked, as she showed them to me.

"Well, yes – and no," she admitted. "They're definitely reminding me what everything looked like, but they've made me realise there's something I totally neglected to do."

I was intrigued. Both my own memory and her photos were serving to confirm that her hard work had been well repaid in the form of both flowers and produce.

So whatever could it be that she felt she had neglected?

"I forgot to pause to look properly and enjoy it all." She smiled. "These photographs are reminding me just how lovely the flowers were, and how well most of my crops did.

"At the time I never stopped long enough to really look and take notice, or even think how wonderful it was that they should have grown from such tiny seeds.

"I do know that I admired things in passing, but rather than rejoice in the moment, I was immediately heading off to tackle the next job. Even when the fruit and vegetables became ready to harvest, I was more concerned about what to do with them than how miraculous it all was.

"I did give a lot away, of course," she continued. "But even then there was a lot left to worry about, and whether to make things into jam or chutney, or if there was a better way I should know about."

I couldn't help laughing, but I did feel her words might well apply to a lot of us, including me.

These days it's well known that gardens are good for both mental and physical health – but only if we allow them to work their magic!

It's when we stop scurrying around that we have the time to realise what things are real and important, and what are merely clouds that will – like all clouds – eventually pass.

What are far more enduring are the sounds of birdsong, the feel of a cool breeze on our face, the taste of a home-grown strawberry, the sight and smell of early honeysuckle.

They're such simple and everyday pleasures that we hardly notice them!

This was brought home to me recently in another way. I was on a shopping trip to my nearest city, and although it has a famous cathedral, I've walked past it so often that I rarely notice it.

This time, mentally preoccupied and mildly impatient with the number of tourists in the way, I had paused only to check my shopping list when one of those tourists turned to me with a smile.

"Beautiful, isn't it?" he said.

I followed his gaze upwards to mellow golden stone, carved angels and apostles, and high towers soaring against a blue sky.

Serene and timeless, it was indeed beautiful, yet it had taken a stranger to bring its loveliness to my attention.

Before I could turn back to agree, he had already been swallowed up by a group of other tourists heading towards the cloisters, but I was nonetheless grateful to him.

His remark had given me a welcome and much-needed prompt that just because something is familiar it doesn't mean we should take it for granted.

Bobbie noticed my abstraction and laughed.

"I hope these photos aren't boring you," she teased.

They hadn't been, of course, and with tea and biscuits to encourage us, it wasn't long before we were back to the business of sorting through those seed catalogues, and discussing just what plant combinations she might try this year.

With decisions made, she sat back with a smile, pushing aside the photos.

"You know," she began, "I'm already looking forward to planting all those spring flowers. But one thing I won't forget this year is to stop and enjoy them."

Now that's an excellent resolution – and one which I, too, am going to adopt! ■

A Year In Nature:
Spring

Fascinating facts about
Bumblebees

■ Two-thirds of the world's crop species rely on pollinators, of which bumblebees are the most important. Birds and butterflies are among the other animals that do the same job, but none as effectively as the humble bee.

■ Their wings beat around 130 times per second. They beat back and forth, rather than up and down, closer to the movement of a helicopter than a bird.

■ Only honey bees die after they sting you – other varieties live on. And males of any bee family can't sting at all!

■ Just 10 per cent of bees live in hives or large social groups. The vast majority of bees are solitary, making their homes in tree trunks or holes in the ground. Some even move into abandoned rodent tunnels.

■ For a long time, bees were thought to be vegetarian, but they actually consume microscopic organisms in the pollen, which means that instead they are classified as omnivorous. Research has proven their young depend on these organisms for survival. Wasps, however, are carnivorous.

Butterfly Thoughts

I've many things to think about
And lots of things to do,
Yet thoughts are like the butterflies
And flit off in the blue.
They take me off to other lands
And places I have been,
To far-off times and happy days
And many things I've seen.
A sea of blue and fields of green
Or playing in the snow,
Then sometimes walking hand in hand
With one I used to know.
Tomorrow I'll begin again,
I'll try another day,
Till then my thoughts are butterflies
And softly flit away.

Iris Hesselden

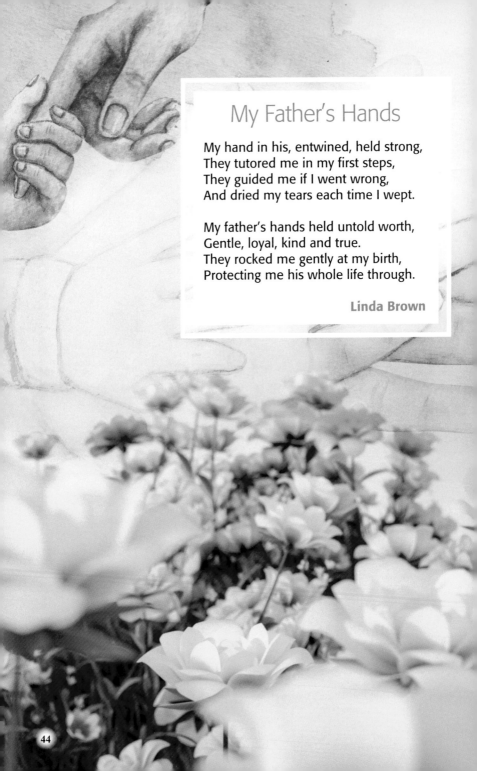

My Father's Hands

My hand in his, entwined, held strong,
They tutored me in my first steps,
They guided me if I went wrong,
And dried my tears each time I wept.

My father's hands held untold worth,
Gentle, loyal, kind and true.
They rocked me gently at my birth,
Protecting me his whole life through.

Linda Brown

Wash Day

Is there anything more pleasing
Than a wash day with some sun?
A gentle breeze, some tuneful birds,
My heart is truly won.
To see the sheets blow white as sails
Is always such a lift,
As a welcome cup of tea
Concludes my laundry shift.

Judy Jarvie

For Ever Sweet

Summer steps out of the wings,
Confident and bright,
A very sunny nature
Welcomed, with delight.
Music of the little birds
On their runway in the skies,
Chirpy, singing in the sun
Their sweet light lullabies.
They love the warmth and freshness,
The scent after the rain,
The trees washed to brightest green
When they fly back home again.
A bouquet of beautiful flowers,
Joyous smiles through the days,
A sigh of butterflies in the heart,
And nectar-perfumed ways.
Pink cerise, the briar roses,
Pretty camellias and sweet peas,
The sunflowers in gorgeous array –
Magic on the breeze.
The loveliness of summertime,
The rainbows and blue skies,
The busy bees and honey teas,
And more, of sweet surprise.

Dorothy McGregor

My Feathered Friends

The happy, hearty blackbird,
Who welcomes me at dawn,
Lifts up my spirit to the sky
On another glorious morn.

The cheerful little robin
Boldly chirps his cheerful song;
His red breast fires my prospect
With the courage to be strong.

The rejoicing of the skylarks
Is sweet and clear above,
When I walk upon the heather
On the mountainside I love.

The haunting hoot of wise old owl,
As dusk surrounds my way,
Reminds me that the darkest night
For some is lightest day!

My favourite is the song thrush
With a melody divine.
Pleasing voices made in heaven,
Those feathered friends of mine!

George Hughes

It's Time

I love where I live,
But I must get away;
I've been here too long,
All work and no play.
The swallows are here;
It's time I was gone.
The cuckoo is calling,
Urging me on.

I want to see places
I've not seen before,
Memories to make
For my winter store.
I want to meet people,
Maybe make a new friend;
I want to take pictures,
Write postcards to send.

The swallows remind me
How swiftly time flies,
So tomorrow I'll wake up
To different blue skies.
It won't be for ever
That I'll be from home,
Just time for releasing
That yearning to roam.

John Darley

A Day In The Sun

The morning sun greets with delight
Every creature in its sight.

The midday sun is hot and bright
And fills the world with warmth and light.

The evening sun bids us goodnight
Then gently blazes out of sight.

Lily Christie

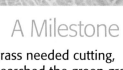

A Milestone

The grass needed cutting,
So I searched the green ground
For lawnmower hazards,
And here's what I found:
A discarded skipping rope,
My daughter's, no less,
And the sight of it there
Set my thoughts to process,
As I suddenly realised
And felt – sadly – resigned
That this showed she was leaving
Her childhood behind.

The grass underneath it
Was now yellow, not green,
Showing how long
And just where it had been.
It may seem to you that
I'm reading too much
In the careless abandonment
Of a plaything, as such.
But we all have our milestones
As we travel life's way,
And I've seen for myself
My daughter's today.

John Darley

Stories By The Shore

I N the words of the ever-popular music hall song, "I belong to Glasgow." I'm very proud to be able to say that Glasgow's my home town and that I'm from the west.

I was born there, in a nursing home on the fringe of the city's Kelvingrove Park. I was educated in Glasgow, first of all at primary school and then at senior school.

I spent many of my childhood days playing in and around Victoria Park, which was adjacent to the west end area of the city where I lived with my family.

Following my school education, I worked for several years in a Glasgow bank before responding to the call to enter the ministry of the Church of Scotland.

To equip me for my future profession in the church, I studied Arts and Divinity at – yes, you've guessed – the University of Glasgow.

I lived out my early years in and around that famous and wonderful Clydeside city.

On reflection, I calculate that I spent the first 32 years of my life in Glasgow. So, by birth, I am a man of the west! However, as life in the ministry progressed, I began to gravitate towards the east.

My first charge was in Alloa, roughly halfway between Glasgow and the Scottish capital, Edinburgh.

Following eight years of ministry in Alloa, I moved north-east to the delightful town of Nairn, which nestles on the shores of the beautiful Moray Firth, where I ministered for a further 25 years.

I retired, again to the east, to the ancient and historic St Andrews, famous for Scotland's oldest university and golf.

In the course of my lifetime, my profession has taken me from my roots in the west of Scotland over to the east of my beloved Scotia.

But during many of my early years in Glasgow, family holidays were regularly spent in the east. To be precise, they were taken on the coast of the East Neuk of Fife.

My late father was Captain of a Glasgow Boys' Brigade Company, which held its annual summer camp on a farm between ▶

iStock

By Rev. Ian W.F. Hamilton.

This four-dial clock stands in Victoria Park, Glasgow.

Anstruther and Pittenweem.

Every year while Dad was at BB camp, my mother, my sister Dianne and myself holidayed in either Anstruther or Pittenweem. We came to know the East Neuk area well over the years, especially those two fishing ports where we holidayed. Never did I think that in my later years I would actually retire to this part of the country.

St Andrews is just a stone's throw from the East Neuk, so, perhaps unconsciously, I had had a taster for my retirement residence in those early exciting childhood years.

I spent much of my childhood holiday time around the harbours at Anstruther and Pittenweem, and I vividly recall jumping on and off the fishing boats tied up there.

As you can imagine, a stroll around those harbours today is like a trip down memory lane every time we visit, and it brings back many delightful childhood memories.

A particular memory I have of my harbourside adventures is collecting and writing down in my "Fishing Boat Scrapbook" the names of the many fishing boats in port, especially at Pittenweem.

The harbour there was, and still is, the fishing centre of the East Neuk, as the fish market is situated on the quayside.

Often the boats in the harbour were berthed three or four deep, so I had plenty vessels to see and plenty names to gather!

I knew I still had that scrapbook somewhere in my study, so recently, following a visit to Pittenweem harbour, I decided to dig it out.

It did take me quite a while to locate it, but as it is written, "Seek and ye shall find". Eventually I did!

On looking at the details I had entered into the book long ago, what immediately struck me was the fact that so many of the vessels had been given names with biblical connotations.

First up was *Galilee*. It reminded me at once of the scene recorded in the gospels down by the Sea of Galilee, where Jesus called four fishermen to become his disciples.

Would you believe the very next name on my boat list was *Disciple*?

Further down the list I encountered *Saviour*, *Launch Out* and *Follow Me*, which is exactly what Jesus told people to do.

Long before entering the ministry, I'd unconsciously collated a series of sermon suggestions, or, if you like, a fishing fleet of summer sermons.

In line with biblical tradition, I'm keeping the best until last.

The final fishing boat I want to extract from my scrapbook is the vessel I discovered, named *Venture Again*.

What an appropriate name to give a fishing boat, I thought. That's exactly what its crew would have had to do, time after time.

Anstruther's harbour, Fife.

Some catches would have been better than others, I imagine, and you know what they say: "If at first you don't succeed . . . venture again!"

Venturing, or trying, again is part and parcel of life.

I'm reminded of Jesus's classic story about the father who had two sons, one of whom ventured out from his home with his share of the family estate tucked into his money belt.

He lived it up and had a ball, to say the least.

But after his money had run out completely, and in a situation of sheer poverty and desperation, realising his folly, he decided to venture home again.

What would the reception be like? At least his father might take him on as a hired servant, he thought.

He needn't have worried.

What a reception! The best robe, the ring, the shoes, the fatted calf and a family party thrown in for good measure.

"Try again, son. You'll do better next time!" is what the forgiving father was saying to his boy.

Jesus's purpose in telling this story is to show just how much our heavenly father gives all of us the opportunity to try and to venture again, that we each may do better next time.

My summer trips to the East Neuk harbours in childhood gave me so much pleasure – and my records of the names of the boats in my "Fishing Boat Scrapbook" will continue to give me much food for thought for the rest of my life. ■

A Year In Nature:

Summer

Fascinating facts about
Seals

■ Britain has two types of seal on its coastline – the harbour seal and the grey seal. Other species have been spotted, but usually only in northern parts of Scotland. Seals generally prefer the colder temperature of northern waters, where they live on the shore, never venturing more than a few miles out to sea.

■ A layer of blubber surrounds seals on the inside, allowing them to withstand waters that hover around freezing. An Icelandic fisherman once survived for six hours in similar conditions after his boat sank. Studies found that his body fat composition resembled that of seals.

■ Seals are thought to have evolved from land mammals. A skeleton found in the north of Canada found a species believed to be the missing link between the two. Badgers and bears are their closest relatives on land.

■ They have a high level of carbon monoxide in their blood because they spend so much time underwater, when they're holding their breath. Only through exhalation can carbon monoxide be released.

■ The Baikal seal exists only in Lake Baikal in Siberia, the world's deepest lake and 395 miles long. They're the only seals to live in an exclusively freshwater environment.

Vanishing Clouds

Like giant marshmallows
They float in the sky,
Fluffy, fat, delicious.

Their changing shapes
A treat for our eyes,
A bird, a beast fictitious.

Till the scorching sun
Melts them away,
A wisp, then gone, capricious.

Lily Christie

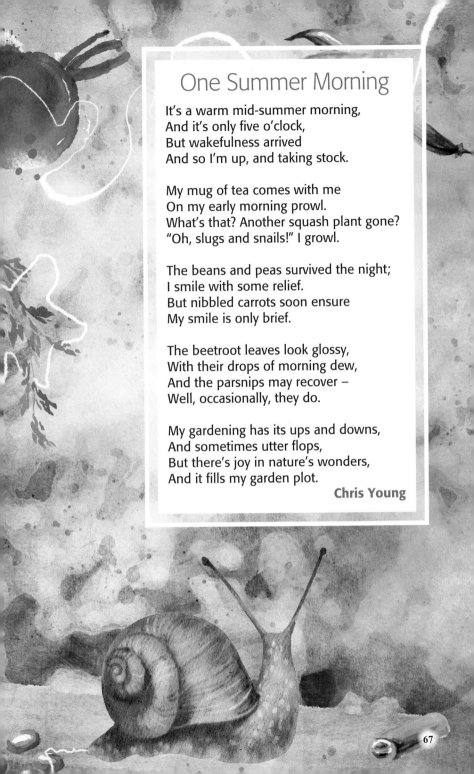

One Summer Morning

It's a warm mid-summer morning,
And it's only five o'clock,
But wakefulness arrived
And so I'm up, and taking stock.

My mug of tea comes with me
On my early morning prowl.
What's that? Another squash plant gone?
"Oh, slugs and snails!" I growl.

The beans and peas survived the night;
I smile with some relief.
But nibbled carrots soon ensure
My smile is only brief.

The beetroot leaves look glossy,
With their drops of morning dew,
And the parsnips may recover –
Well, occasionally, they do.

My gardening has its ups and downs,
And sometimes utter flops,
But there's joy in nature's wonders,
And it fills my garden plot.

Chris Young

Away Day

Let's go down to the seaside –
The weather looks set to be fine.
We'll paddle and play
In the shallows all day
With your hand tucked safely in mine.

Come with me down to the seaside.
There's so much that waits to be done:
Rock pools to explore
Castles, swimming and more
While we're kissed by the warmth of the sun.

Shall we dine down by the seaside?
Alfresco food always tastes best:
Chips and fried fish,
Eat as much as we wish –
The seagulls will finish the rest.

Let's stroll down by the seaside
When the sun's setting, orangey-red,
Then home we will go,
Worn out but aglow,
Full of memories and ready for bed.

Laura Tapper

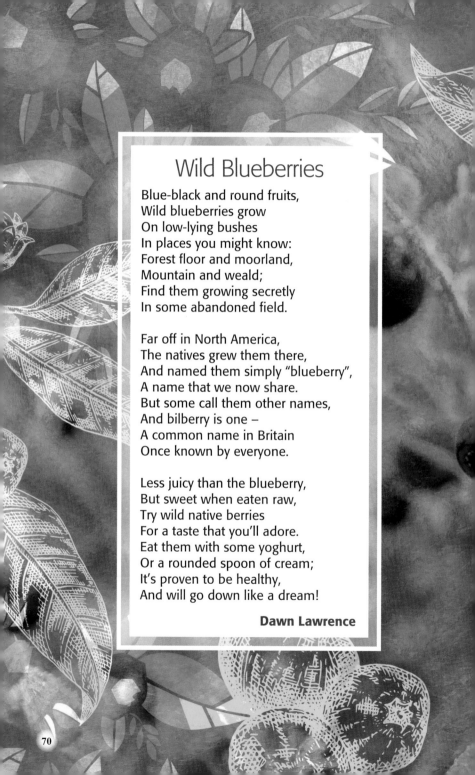

Wild Blueberries

Blue-black and round fruits,
Wild blueberries grow
On low-lying bushes
In places you might know:
Forest floor and moorland,
Mountain and weald;
Find them growing secretly
In some abandoned field.

Far off in North America,
The natives grew them there,
And named them simply "blueberry",
A name that we now share.
But some call them other names,
And bilberry is one –
A common name in Britain
Once known by everyone.

Less juicy than the blueberry,
But sweet when eaten raw,
Try wild native berries
For a taste that you'll adore.
Eat them with some yoghurt,
Or a rounded spoon of cream;
It's proven to be healthy,
And will go down like a dream!

Dawn Lawrence

In The Country

From the heat of August I have shied
And walk the lane this cooler side;
From here I see the fields of wheat
Standing tall, their growth complete.
We're coming to that time of year
When harvesting draws ever near,
But, just for now, peace reigns supreme
And time drifts by as in a dream.
These lazy, summer, salad days
Show all that's best of country ways.

John Darley

That Summer

By then six weeks of bright sky
Had left the land for dead;
The days breathless and their long light
Flickering the fields to whitest gold.

At night the wide-open window,
The maroon night full of furry moths –
Of such a still warmth
I woke and slept and woke.

I didn't want the others; hadn't learnt their language –
Wasn't interested in mornings
Spinning bicycles down lanes to laughing woods –
I was content with quiet.

One day I knew the only thing I wanted:
I walked over fields that crackled
Through an air that tasted dusty yellow,
Searching thirsty for the river.

I saw it like a glass slide,
Most of it gone to great white beaches.
And there beyond, one cauldron of a pool,
Dark and deep in smoky quartz.

I stripped, wobbled over stones,
Let the delicious silk of water
Sink around my neck.
I closed my eyes and treaded blue-white cool.

Kenneth Steven

Moonlit Meditation

Come with me on a moonlit walk
On a night so still and calm.
We'll leave the city far behind,
Discover healing balm.
And soon we'll pause to see the stars,
They set the sky alight;
They touch our minds with wonder
And fill us with delight.

Then, as the clouds all drift away,
We watch the moon appear,
So magical and beautiful,
She seems so very near.
We feel that time is standing still;
Enchantment fills the air.
Peace, which passes understanding,
All round us everywhere.

Our walk has brought us hope and joy,
Our worries far away;
We'll keep this magic in our hearts
To help us through the day.

Iris Hesselden

Time To Flourish

THIS year I planted a new flower-bed in my garden. In the past I've relied on sowing annual seeds and the outcome hasn't always been satisfactory, but this year I was able to afford to buy plants, and the resulting summer display was amazing: a geum that didn't stop flowering, fabulous foxgloves, a glorious purple lupin, pinks and sweet Williams, a wild mallow.

My roses are always superb every year, and the seeds I did plant – poppies, cornflowers, cosmos, sweet peas – flourished, too.

Summer brings the fulfilment of the expectation we had when we planted in the spring. We would be very disappointed if our gardens remained fallow after all the work we've done.

In our spiritual lives, too, we expect to see some blossoming of loveliness – if we say we follow Christ then there needs to be some evidence to back that up.

To use a different metaphor, Jesus talked about good trees bearing good fruit and said that the branches that don't bear fruit are cut off and useful for nothing but burning.

There was an occasion when he cursed an olive tree because it bore no fruit and it shrivelled up and died.

Some of us might worry about the lack of blossoming in our lives. We feel that we're not good enough, that there isn't much evidence of loveliness.

To that I say that we are all works in progress and that it takes time to grow, just as we have to wait for the summer to produce blossom and fragrance.

Paul wrote to the Philippians, "Continue to work out your salvation with fear and trembling, for it is God who works in you to will and to act according to his good purpose."

They hadn't arrived. Nor had Paul himself, as he says later in his letter when he talks of how he longs to be found in Christ, how he wants to know the power of his resurrection, to share in ▶

iStock.

By Rev. Susan Sarapuk.

his sufferings and to attain the resurrection from the dead.

We already have our salvation – that's something Christ won for us on the cross – but now it needs to be worked out. We need to grow in understanding, in knowledge and in the works of God. But we don't do it alone.

God is at work in us to make it happen because it's what he wants. It's not a matter of trying our hardest to please him – it's working with him in the power of the Holy Spirit.

I became a Christian when I was a student. Friends took me to a special invitation service at All Souls, Langham Place. I didn't know that was their plan when they invited me to tea, and I didn't want to be there.

But that evening, as I experienced the worship and heard the Bible expounded, I responded in repentance and faith.

The next few months were the most wonderful, exhilarating time I'd ever experienced in my life.

The nearest thing you could compare it to is being madly in love. I was in love with Jesus, bursting with joy every day, eager to love and serve people and bring them into the kingdom. I thought it would never come to an end.

But it did; the honeymoon always ends. The intense feelings faded; doubts crept in. I asked myself where all the joy had gone. Was there something wrong with me? Was there some secret sin? Was I losing my faith?

Then I heard another sermon based on this verse, "Being confident of this, that he who began a good work in you will carry it on to completion until the day of Christ Jesus."

I realised that it was God who had called me by his grace and mercy when I wasn't even looking for him. He began the work in me. His promise is that he will finish it.

I'm not doing this on my own. We learn to trust Christ as we grow. Trials are part of life. When we feel far from God, when we feel unworthy, when we feel we've let him down and we are not as good as we should be, that's the time to repent, say we're sorry, get up and start walking again in his strength as we work with the Holy Spirit.

"So I say live by the Spirit," Paul writes to the Galatians.

If you do you will produce love, joy, peace, patience, kindness, goodness, faithfulness, gentleness and self-control, along with all the other Christ-like qualities, the flowering of what was planted in the beginning.

It does not come straight away; it's not a supernatural spell that gives us all these attributes in a flash. We have to endure and grow, steadily and faithfully.

"I have learned to be content whatever the circumstances," Paul wrote.

He knew what it was to be in need and he knew what it was like to have plenty. Through everything, he'd learned to be content in Christ, who gave him the strength for everything.

We don't have instant fullness. We grow as we work out our salvation, knowing that God works with us and in us to fulfil his purposes, knowing that he will finish what he's started.

That gives me confidence and peace and a sense of purpose in my life.

Like a highly scented summer garden, I want to grow into the fullness of Christ, to reflect him. I'll finish by quoting Paul again: "Thanks be to God, who always leads us in triumphal procession in Christ, and through us spreads everywhere the fragrance of the knowledge of him." ■

A Year In Nature:
Summer

Fascinating facts about
Butterflies

■ With taste buds on their feet, butterflies can tell if something is food for them simply by landing on it. They also smell with their feet, so if they sense something tasty they'll then use their proboscis to dig in and eat.

■ Their lives are fleeting, lasting only three to four weeks in butterfly form. The Brimstone butterfly, however, can live up to 13 months. Brimstones do well in modern Britain, and have been on the increase in the last 50 years.

■ Rather than two wings, butterflies have four. If you watch them fly in slow motion, their forewings and hindwings move slightly separately when they're in the air.

■ The Painted Lady variety is capable of making a round trip of about 8,000 miles when it migrates to Europe from Saharan Africa and back again during its life. Conditions in the desert have to be favourable, which is why numbers of them seen in the UK can fluctuate so much from year to year.

■ One of the rarest species, the Miami Blue, is found only in southern Florida, around Miami especially. Development of the city has threatened its survival, as have the area's occasional tropical storms and hurricanes. However, a breeding programme running since 2003 has already made strides towards ensuring its future.

August

It was a long way to the end of summer:
The single-track bump of an ancient track
To a cottage full of butterflies and dust.

After weeks without rain the streams had trickled
To little flickers in among the stones,
Lost whispers that had nothing to say.

And then that night the sky bruised:
The air hung still and the midges danced –
I stood on the back steps holding my breath.

As far away as it was possible to see
A flicker of lightning like a lizard's tongue:
The answering grumble of thunder.

And my sister took me for a drive in the car
As the whole world flickered and roared,
And the rain came down in silver.

The banks gushed water and the river below
Turned a swirling brown in the trees
Like a snake on its way to the sea.

And the following day it was autumn:
The wide skies torn between blue and white
And the last of the storm washed away.

Kenneth Steven

Witness

The wild moor, the fresh bracing air,
The freedom to roam at will,
The winding roads and high hills –
All this heaven our hearts fill.
The curlew glides and soars above,
His warbling cry carried far,
He laps the pebble-bed waters
And follows his own timeless star.
Little minnows swim in the sunlight,
A trout does a twirl in the air –
We're taking wonderful snapshots.
All life is happily there.

Pretty paths of purple-clad heather,
The gorse shining gold after rain,
The sheep quietly grazing,
Just turning to look – in disdain.
The wild moor, untapped, remote,
Yet little tell-tale signs appear,
Sprigs of crocuses and daffodils,
Autumn red, and then winter drear.
We're witness to these awesome ranges,
The low mountains, bringing peace and calm;
The joy of the changing seasons
The moor's mystery, and beauty and charm.

Dorothy McGregor

Recollection

The roses may be past their best
As autumn's presence starts to show,
But here's one that my nose caressed,
Its scent not letting summer go.

Though autumn heralds shorter days
To bring an end to summer's reign,
The roses' scented sweetness stays,
Recalling those hot days again.

John Darley

Thoughts Golden

There are changes afoot, the trees tell us so,
And all is lamplight and flame.
A season of harvest, the gifts of ripe fruit,
How lovely to see you again.
Time honoured music, the snapping of twigs
And the smoke does its signature swirl;
The fires are flaring, the conkers drop down,
A special time for each boy and girl.

Here by the fire is a warm cosy glow,
With a choice tray of nuts and red wine,
The moments are tranquil, reflective, and
In armchair-ad slippers, divine.
The trees are beautiful, a wealth of gold,
And russet and buff, on the bough.
The winds are wrestling with the leaves –
How glorious – the autumn time now.

Dorothy McGregor

Acorn Time

Before the trees have lost their leaves,
September time of year,
The sound of acorns pattering down
Is one we daily hear.
Living close beside a wood
Is like a battle zone;
We're fired upon from right and left,
With bullets hard as stone
Pinging on our window-panes,
Rattling on our door,
Flying down on people's heads
Which often makes them sore.
Plop! Plop! Plop! When winds are high,
And even when they're not,
Our house is showered with acorns,
We wade through quite a lot!
So though our oak trees give us joy,
We love and hold them dear,
We're glad when acorn time has passed
And comes but once a year!

Dawn Lawrence

A Busy Life For Me

I'm sure I shouldn't need to run
Like this, at nearly sixty-one;
I should have cancelled volunteering,
Taken time for make-up, earrings,
Arrived a stately, graceful gran,
In clouds of perfume, a bright kaftan,
Accepting compliments, sitting serene
On a front-row seat, for the first scene.

But as for today, I run through the gate,
Race up the path, with a, "Sorry I'm late!"
Stand at the back of the primary school hall,
Gasping for breath, I lean back on the wall.
Then Isla appears with her face-splitting grin,
Delivers her lines and holds up her chin,
Spots me and waves, brings a tear to my eye –
It's better than spare time, or things I could buy.

And afterwards, when I am making her tea,
She says she was nervous, until she saw me;
By just being there I'd made everything fine –
Would I come to assembly tomorrow, half-nine?

Chris Young

White-tailed Eagle

With steely eyes he stares below,
Where far deep shadows come and go.
His form scarce moves; he stops to pause,
Grasping the crag with fearsome claws;
Then drops – with deadly aim so true,
So quick one's glance can scarce pursue.
And like a thunderbolt he brings
An instant death to those on wings,
Or pounces on some bird or hare,
That ventured out to loiter there.
And rising thermals bring to view
Hawk and kestrel, osprey, too;
So effortless they move and glide,
The eye sees nothing else beside.
But none can fly as high as he,
Who holds command on land and sea:
A white-tailed eagle – powerful, swift,
Is one of nature's rarest gifts.

Dawn Lawrence

Highland

All childhood I would be out at dawn
And up like a kite into the woods;
It was running the hill until breathless
To stand under scurrying skies;
It was being in the woods and listening
To the roaring of great trees beneath.

The woodland was badgers and a hiding of owls;
It was the blue screech of jays and the joy
Of deer battling our over the fields.
It was the knowledge inside that all this was a gift
That got bigger the further you went.

Kenneth Steven

Let Nothing Go To Waste

WHEN you think of autumn, what is the first thing that comes into your mind?

Memories of falling leaves turning familiar paths into streets of gold?

Apples, fresh picked from the tree and still warm from the sun?

Bonfires at dusk, sending sparks dancing upwards into a blue sky?

Or could it be vinegar?

I must admit I had to double check when my friend Sam chanced to mention that the smell of vinegar was one of his earliest and most abiding memories of the season.

"My grandma," he explained, "was a great one for not letting food go to waste.

"Sensible, of course, but it did mean that many of my childhood memories are of Gran making chutney or pickles.

"She had a small orchard in her garden, so every autumn my brother and I would always be sent to pick up all the windfall apples.

"My older sister would be in the kitchen chopping onions, and Gran would be weighing and measuring all the other ingredients.

"Quite a lot of those chopped apples and sultanas found their way into our mouths rather than into the mixture, but there were still plenty left for the preserves.

"And once all the pans were bubbling away, the smell of vinegar and spices was quite inescapable.

"In fact, it seemed to linger for days." He grinned. "All the same, she did make the most wonderful chutney. Plenty for us, and plenty for her neighbours, too.

"Not to mention all kinds of jam and sauces, which were equally delicious. I still can't smell vinegar without thinking of autumn."

I like the sound of Sam's gran.

Making use of produce that might otherwise go to waste is not only sensible, if it becomes a team effort then it can be fun as well.

It's plain that, although she might not have known it, when Gran was making her chutney and jam, she wasn't just preserving food, she was preserving happy memories that have lasted Sam a lifetime. ▶

By Maggie Ingall.

It's strange how the impulse to preserve seems to be an intrinsic part of human nature.

When it comes to food, it's understandable.

In centuries past, the need to keep food in an edible state for both ourselves and our livestock would not just have been desirable, but would have truly made the difference between life or death.

But what about when it comes to preserving other things?

After all, it isn't going to jeopardise our survival if we don't keep that box of shells from a holiday, or the pile of postcards we once loved to collect.

Or even that pretty teacup on the shelf, the sole survivor of the first set we ever owned.

And it's a very rare person who never keeps a favourite book, or a few photos to remind them of times gone by.

Even if we rarely look at them, it's nice to know that we still have them!

A difficulty arises when that need to preserve things from the past actually prevents us from moving towards the future.

"Change is inevitable," was an adage I once read, "except from vending machines."

That sting in the tail still makes me smile, but doesn't stop me from knowing that the truest part of that sentence is undoubtedly the first.

Change is inevitable. It's built into every part of our universe, and our lives are no exception – no matter how welcome or unwelcome change can be.

Often, of course, it's a bit of both.

We can take pleasure in getting a new job, whilst still regretting many aspects of the old one.

We can rejoice in seeing our children achieve independence, whilst still feeling sad that they have left the nest.

But when we can't bear to part with anything, then we can really make life difficult for ourselves.

A few months ago I helped Sandra move from her house into a smaller and more manageable ground-floor flat.

It was exactly what she had wanted, and she was eager to move in — yet when it came to the actual practicalities of packing up, things were going badly awry.

With a lifetime's worth of keepsakes and mementoes to be squeezed into only half the space, she knew there would be no room to take all of them.

Sandra was becoming increasingly bogged down by having to make choices on what to leave behind.

Happily, after a few days of head scratching, we were able to resolve things.

A few very special mementoes were kept, while the majority, less precious to her, were disposed of in other ways.

I went to visit her soon after she moved in.

Everything had been nicely arranged around her rooms or put neatly away, and it was looking beautiful.

Over a celebratory cake, I asked her — not without a little trepidation — if she was still comfortable with the decisions I had helped her to make.

"More than comfortable," she reassured me with a smile. "It might sound strange, but I feel a bit lighter now, if you know what I mean.

"It's just as if all that clutter was literally weighing me down.

"For a very long time I'd been telling myself that I needed all my keepsakes to remind me of just who I was, and what I'd done with my life.

"But of course it turned out that I didn't. I'm still me and I still have all my memories. And I've realised now that the best place to keep them is in my heart and in my head!"

Well said, Sandra, for where else can we store our memories so that they stay for ever fresh and green?

They may not be preserved in jars of vinegar in the same way as Sam's gran so prudently preserved her pickles and chutneys, but whatever season of the year it happens to be, they will be there waiting for us, as fresh and as sweet as they ever were. ■

A Year In Nature:

Autumn

Fascinating facts about
Hedgehogs

■ In the Middle Ages, hedgehogs were known as "urchins" or "urcheons". This is how the sea urchin got its name. The history of the word "urchin" goes back through old French to the Latin *hericius* for hedgehog.

■ Hedgehogs have a top speed of about four miles per hour! That's moving at full pelt, though. They normally wander around one to two miles at night whilst foraging for food.

■ One of the reasons cat and dog food is recommended for leaving out for them is that they're actually lactose-intolerant. Milk does not agree with their digestive system – nor does bread. Insects, slugs and beetles are their wild food of choice.

■ Only a few of the Scottish islands don't have a resident population. Upland areas and dense pine plantations lack suitable nesting grounds and food, but hedgehogs cope quite well in towns and cities, providing they can roam around.

■ With between 5,000 and 7,000 spines on their body, hedgehogs roll into a spiky ball to protect themselves and also to sleep. They are one of only three species in the United Kingdom that hibernate over the winter.

Trick Or Treat

Through theatrical make-up, my reflection winks back
As I practise my cackle and straighten my hat.
My warts look realistic, I'll just add one more,
Then top up the sweets in the dish by the door.
A carved jack-o-lantern shines bright on the path,
To greet costumed families as they wander past.
I've plenty of treats for the children's delight,
But first, just for fun, why not give them a fright?

Laura Tapper

Romance And Fireworks

November's cloud
Is raining stars –
Pink, purple, green and gold.

And as they fall
And fade away
We hug against the cold.

Michelle Illing

Amongst The Poppies

Once again we stand in silence,
Amongst the poppies red and warm,
Vowing always to remember,
Those who saved us from the storm,
Those who gave their lives in war,
That we in freedom might grow old.
Poppies will give way to holly,
And our remembrance won't grow cold.

George Hughes

To A Candle

From a tiny spark you waken,
Red your core that turns to gold;
Growing in the air that feeds you,
Eager, trembling, greedy, bold.
Lighting up the inky darkness,
Twisting, twirling to and fro,
Like a dancer pirouetting,
Shivering slightly as you grow.

What excitement – what a flurry,
Chasing shadows over walls,
Lighting up the hidden corners
Where your warming radiance falls.
A sudden light to pierce the darkness,
Like some tropic forest flower;
A little life that looms and lingers,
Burning bright for many an hour.

I have watched you falter, flutter,
With the merest breath that blows,
But the spark that's lit within you
Simply strengthens, grows and grows.
As I contemplate that radiance
Caught within your trance-like beam,
I see the world as once imagined,
Softly mirrored through a dream.

And with my sense of new awakening,
All those phantoms once so feared,
Fade, like all encroaching shadows,
And in your light have disappeared.

Dawn Lawrence

After The Deluge

The air seemed heavy, ominous,
The sky grew dark, as dark as night;
It seemed the whole world held its breath
As it awaited nature's might.
And then those dark skies opened wide
And emptied out torrential rain
Which flooded gutters, battered trees,
And overflowed each leaf-filled drain.
Shop windows took a battering,
Rain hammering like a power jet,
And shoppers huddled miserably
In every doorway, dripping wet.
And then, as swiftly as it came,
The downpour stopped and all was calm,
All eyes turned upwards to the skies,
While some held out a hopeful palm.
The sky now glowed bright peach and pink,
The brightest sky I've ever seen,
So peaceful and benevolent
As if the rain had never been!

Eileen Hay

The Mug Cupboard

The cupboard near my kettle is extremely tightly packed!
I've mugs of all varieties – some new, some old and cracked.
I've every size and colour, so which do I like to use?
Well, depending on the time, it isn't difficult to choose!

So first thing in the morning it's my old rose-patterned cup –
It's large, you see – I need a lot of tea to wake me up!
And then, around eleven, when I take a little break,
The dainty daisy mug's just right for coffee with my cake.

My lunchtimes can be leisurely, a good time to unwind,
So I settle with a cuppa and a thoughtful frame of mind.
I like to reminisce on holidays of bygone years,
So I use one of the many mugs I've bought as souvenirs!

I love my afternoon tea and I'll often have a guest,
So out will come the matching set of mugs I keep for best.
Or if I'm feeling swanky, I'll bring out the china pot
With cups and saucers, milk jug, fancy sugar tongs – the lot!

But bedtime means hot chocolate time, then I've a choice of three,
And they're the very special mugs that loved ones gave to me.
Each one will guarantee my day a warm, uplifting end.
They're the ones that say "Best Mum", "Best Nan" or
   "For A Special Friend".

Emma Canning

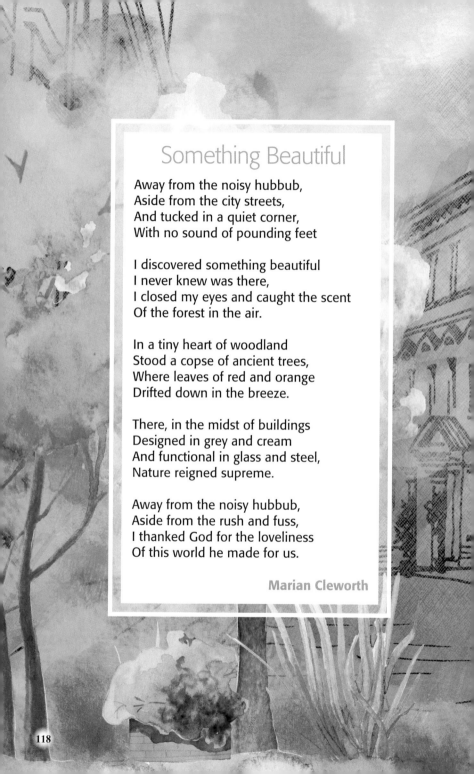

Something Beautiful

Away from the noisy hubbub,
Aside from the city streets,
And tucked in a quiet corner,
With no sound of pounding feet

I discovered something beautiful
I never knew was there,
I closed my eyes and caught the scent
Of the forest in the air.

In a tiny heart of woodland
Stood a copse of ancient trees,
Where leaves of red and orange
Drifted down in the breeze.

There, in the midst of buildings
Designed in grey and cream
And functional in glass and steel,
Nature reigned supreme.

Away from the noisy hubbub,
Aside from the rush and fuss,
I thanked God for the loveliness
Of this world he made for us.

Marian Cleworth

In Full Flight

I WAS fortunate to grow up in a small rural community on the Solway Firth.

As a child there was great freedom to play in parks and woods, to cycle along quiet country roads, to paddle and skim stones in the river, and to explore the sandy pools of the nearby seaside.

Perhaps that's one reason I have always loved birds. My memories of those lazy, hazy days of childhood summers always include a variety of birdsong.

I remember a blackbird who built her nest among the climbing roses in our back yard. Her early morning song was full of joy and enthusiasm for a new day.

There were various small birds that flitted among the trees in our favourite wood – blue tits, coal tits, robins and sparrows.

The joy of hearing the drumming of a woodpecker and being rewarded with a streak of black, red and white as it darted past!

On the river were swans, dippers and even a kingfisher.

My memories of the Solway shores are the most precious.

In the summer, this vast, sandy shoreline is amass with pink thrift, alive with the "peewit" call of lapwing and the warble of the lark.

Larks were always difficult to see on the ground, their streaky brown bodies easily camouflaged, but the minute they rose, their vertical flight and warbling song of pure summer gladness made them instantly recognisable.

P.B. Shelley could find nothing with which to compare that "unbodied joy".

In the late autumn the skies over the Solway are filled with the honking of thousands of geese flying in on that wonderful V formation from the Arctic.

The entire population of geese from one island group in the Arctic comes to the salt marshes of the Solway to winter.

I have often wondered whether geese honk continually through their flight, or whether the leader at the front sets them all off with excitement when he spies the well-known landscape below ▶

By Janice Ross.

iStock.

120

and realises they are nearly home.

Some readers will have been blessed with parents or grandparents who were keen birdwatchers. Many youngsters will have learned to stay very still and silent while watching some rare specimen that brings a few minutes of shared joy before flitting off again.

Many will have memories of camping out in hides for the whole day with gloves, scarf and hat pulled firmly down and a promised flask of hot chocolate, just to catch a glimpse of an elusive bird.

Many will remember the blast of the keen north wind whistling through the hide's viewing slit.

Alan McFadyen was one such youngster.

"I remember my grandfather taking me to see the kingfisher nest, and I just remember being completely blown away by how magnificent the birds are," he said.

He became an avid wildlife photographer, returning to the same spot to photograph the kingfishers.

After six years, 4,200 hours and 720,000 photos, he captured a perfect shot of a kingfisher diving straight into the water without a single splash. What an awesome photograph!

For my oldest granddaughter, it is a memory of standing at the back door of our home in Orkney one October morning, wrapped in a warm rug, watching as a huge flock of loudly cackling geese flew overhead.

She was not quite three at the time, but the wonder has never left her.

Perhaps it was the explosion of sound coupled with the awesome sight of hundreds of great birds flying in formation that so firmly imprinted the occasion in her mind.

As autumn closes in, we will have said farewell to our swallow and housemartin friends as they seek warmer climes, and we will become increasingly aware of visitors from Scandinavia and Greenland pouring in.

The yearly flight of migratory birds is surely one of the amazing works of God's creation.

In his excellent book, "In The Beginning Was Information", Dr Werner Gitt explains two miracles required in migation: energy and navigation.

One of the problems facing a migratory bird is that of taking off with sufficient fuel or fat to complete the whole journey. Just as excess baggage is not allowed on an aeroplane, so a bird must be light to fly well.

But then, as many migratory birds don't even make a "pit stop" on their travels, they have to have enough fuel to complete the journey. A bird also needs to know the most economical cruising speed: not too slow or he will run out on the way; not too fast as that would mean using up energy battling air resistance.

The question has to be asked: how does the bird know all this?

Dr Gitt gives a fascinating example of the golden plover, which migrates from Alaska to Hawaii for the summer, travelling non-stop on a 4,000 km flight over open sea. There is nowhere for this bird to land for a rest on its 88-hour journey and it cannot swim.

The bird somehow puts on precisely the right amount and concentration of fat it needs.

Studies of this little bird – charting its starting weight, the fat stored for fuel, and the rate of use of fat reserves throughout the flight – discovered that, at 800 km from the end of its flight, the bird would crash into the sea!

Dr Gitt believes that God gave this little bird an important piece of information on conserving energy: "Do not fly singly, but in a V formation".

So the bird arrives safely, with the added miracle of 6.8 g of fat in hand, which might have been needed for a contrary wind.

For those eager to discover what information God gave to birds on navigation, I recommend that you read this fascinating book.

So, dear reader, as you are alerted to the arrival of our honking friends on our shores this autumn, may you think about the awesome "information" that God has installed in his beautiful creation, and pause to meditate on the wonders of God's works around us. ■

A Year In Nature:
Autumn

Fascinating facts about
Squirrels

■ After a busy year of storing and hiding food for winter, squirrels can sniff it out even under about a foot of snow. They then tunnel down to retrieve it, too, which is useful as they lose roughly a quarter of their food to other animals – including other squirrels!

■ Our beloved native reds don't just live in the UK. They're spread across Europe and beyond into Mongolia and parts of China. Reds are more active at dawn and dusk, so that's the best time to spot them.

■ Red squirrels can be left- or right-handed – or even ambidextrous. If they're eating a pinecone, spot which side the top is pointing. A left-handed squirrel's will be pointing left, and vice-versa.

■ In case of emergencies, squirrels build more than one nest (called a drey). If one comes under attack from predators or suffers weather damage, they have another cosy home ready and waiting for them and their kittens.

■ It's not entirely true that grey squirrels conquered the UK single-handedly after being brought from the States by the Victorians. Well-to-do landowners would share out squirrels across the country, so it's more to do with our behaviour than theirs. In 2010, one grey was found to have unwittingly nestled under a warm car bonnet in Glasgow and ended up being taken to the Isle of Skye!

Shutterstock

One Stitch, Two Stitch

Knit one, purl one,
Click, click, click,
Needles flashing
Deft and quick.

Knit one, purl one,
Slowly grows,
Stitch by stitch,
That's how it goes.

You drop a stitch
And you go wrong,
You pick it up
And carry on.

It takes time
And patience, too,
Calms you down,
Pleasant to do.

Choosing wool
Is a real delight;
A finished knit
Such a lovely sight.

It's cold out there
Not always fair,
But I'm happy to sit
And quietly knit.

Tina Cathleen MacNaughton

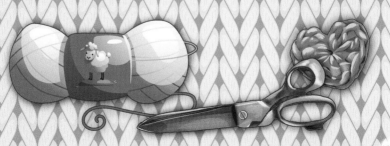

Unchanging Times

The town's old clock sedately stands,
Passing time with steady hands.
Its face set in a 12-foot tower
Shows, to all, each passing hour.

Unveiled in eighteen ninety-three,
The mayor himself turned first its key.
A crowd, assembled, gave applause,
Approving of this worthy cause.

It stands, a landmark, on the street,
A place where lovers used to meet.
Some had looked up anxiously,
Wondering where their love could be.

It's kept time through the years and reigns,
The wars, the peace, the losses, gains.
And though, today, life seems a race
Its hands still move at its own pace.

Despite the efforts of mankind,
Seeking ways to shorten time,
The clock continues to this day
To tick the same old hours away.

John Darley

Autumn Sunset

Light, glorious radiant light,
That blazes in the sky,
Bright lilac, crimson, peach,
Enchanting to the eye.
Ploughed fields, the old church tower
All seem to be ablaze,
Lit by the dazzling sky's
Sublime celestial rays.
Time, ever moving time,
Decrees that this must end,
Such beauty must be brief
And chill dark night descend.

Eileen Hay

Oh, Look!

Winter's wearing white this year –
What a welcoming surprise
To see again the fresh bright snow,
Pirouetting before our eyes.

Sparkling diamonds all her own
Are strewn across the land,
A finely frosted filigree
Sewn by an icy hand.

The waist-coated little robin
Perches on the freezing bough.
We smile at his bright touch of red,
Bringing magic to us now.

Then on the evergreen we see
Coronets of ice, aglow,
Passing by a moment,
They could be white roses in the
   snow.

This glacial, pure heaven,
Layer on layer, lighting the ways;
Winter's wearing white this year,
Casting her spell, on the wonderland
   ways.

Dorothy McGregor

Mistletoe

Oh, little bough of mistletoe, are you just
   for Christmas kisses? No.
I came upon you growing free, clinging to
   an old oak tree.
With your shiny leaves and berries white,
   in your natural place you looked just right.
I know I could have cut you down, wrapped
   a bright red ribbon round
And hung you up above my door, for
   decoration, nothing more.
There'll be kisses enough on Christmas Day,
   so I leave you be and walk away.
Up high in the winter branches bare, you do
   look rather splendid there.

Vivien Brown

Christmas Joy

How wonderful the Christmas cards
With pictures of the snow,
Kiddies sledding, snowball throwing,
All the world aglow.
A stunning panorama,
A brilliant delight,
The heavens overflowing
With dazzling signs of white.
The essence is the silence
As the snow tumbles down,
While covered in the blanket
The little animals gone to ground.
We see now the Victorians
Skated on frozen ponds,
Footman, coach and horses,
Piano nights and song,
Diamonds glistening in the snow,
The skies mother-of-pearl,
The horizon disappearing
In mists of glacial swirl.
Lamplight and carolling
Goodwill spread on the ice,
And which we save of the Christmas cards —
Is the throw of winter's dice.

Dorothy McGregor

Memories

Christmas presents sealed and wrapped,
Excitement greets the dawn.
Squeals of joy and great delight
Ring through the Christmas morn.

Winter spice, aromas sweet
Permeate the air;
Friends and family gather,
But not everyone is there.

The years race by relentlessly,
But memories lock down tight
Of ones we've said goodbye to
On our darkest tear-stained night.

Across the years at Christmas
Those memories still burn bright:
The beauty of our loved ones
At peace and sleeping tight.

But the Morning Star of Christmas
Has light enough to throw
On all your secret sorrow,
More than you can know.

The heart of God will hold you;
He knows just what to do.
He is the Christmas Story
And today he's here for you.

Karen Stokes

139

Twelfth Night Reflections

We decked all the halls in excitement,
With holly, and lights and a tree;
We counted the days throughout Advent,
Consuming mince-pies with our tea.

We loved the Nine Lessons and Carols
In the small village kirk down the road;
We greeted our friends with a warm "Merry Christmas"
When out for a walk in the cold.

The children, how their eyes sparkled,
When, at last, Christmas Day came around.
They opened their gifts in such wonder,
Pulled crackers, ate lunch wearing crowns.

Yet soon it becomes but a memory,
Quite precious, held close to the heart;
We smile whilst rereading the cards we take down,
Admiring a child's festive art.

And finally, down comes the Christmas tree,
The room will look bare, but it's time
To pack baubles in age-faded boxes.
Oh, look! A missed chocolate. That's mine!

Chris Young

from the Manse Window

A Moment's Peace

W HEN travelling internationally you are generally insulated from the elements – by shuttle buses, travelators, air conditioning, covered accessways – but sometimes the weather makes its presence felt.

Flying home from America is always an emotional wrench for us. We leave behind one much-loved set of grandchildren and fly towards the others.

The weather forecast was dubious, but the tickets were booked, and we didn't want to apply for citizenship!

The local flight into Philadelphia was fine – although I couldn't help smiling when I found we were sharing that tiny aircraft with a basketball team, not one of whom was under seven feet tall!

The change-over to a bigger plane took two hours, but those hours were insulated ones. Anything happening outside passed us on by.

Then it was off to Atlanta. Amidst that enormous urban sprawl, the pilot found the airport and our second transfer, an Airbus to Amsterdam.

But before we could take off, we had to be defrosted.

Or, rather, the Airbus had to be defrosted.

With all the passengers on board, two trucks with hydraulic platforms and hoses on the back sprayed us from tip to tail with a high-pressure de-icing fluid.

It was like being in a car wash – but in a plane!

The transatlantic leg was mostly spent tucked under a blanket.

It was a good job we got some rest on the plane, because things would go awfully wrong at Schiphol in Amsterdam.

The weather was so bad with snow and ice that planes were landing, only to be parked.

We disembarked, along with many other planeloads of people, to be told there would be no flights out – to anywhere – for the next three days!

The queues of people looking for rooms in ▶

iStock.

By David McLaughlan.

142

Amsterdam soon outstripped availability. The help-desk workers gave up and went home.

Not knowing the city at all, my sweetheart and I were faced with the option of the most expensive rooms – a suite – in the Schiphol Hilton – or three days and two nights in the airport corridors.

With a shudder of trepidation, I presented the credit card.

Safely in our suite, breathing a sigh of relief because we had a bed at least, the next problem reared its head.

We had no idea where our luggage was!

Still, the suite was lovely! Looking out through diamond-shaped windows, we saw an actual winter wonderland. Just not one we wanted to venture out into.

For the next three days we stayed in the suite, with occasional trips to the airport shops to buy essentials.

Our normally hectic schedules, with work and babysitting grandchildren, were absolutely on hold.

Television soon lost its charm compared to the view from the top of the Hilton tower.

We took to spending time cuddled in, like Beatrix Potter characters in winter.

We talked. Issues that had been privately worrying each of us were resolved.

We gave a lot of thanks. And, miracle of miracles, with all the distractions of modern life stripped away, we found we liked simply being together.

We came out of the experience better than we went in. It was everything a retreat ought to be.

Except, as is so often the case, we needed to be forced into it.

When the weather cleared and planes took to the sky again, we threw ourselves back into the hustle and bustle.

It's almost an illness of modern life that, even after experiencing the benefits of a little seclusion, we so often feel guilty about it and try not to do it again.

Why? The animals Beatrix Potter drew would mostly hibernate for part of the year.

Much of the holiday industry is based on "getting away from it all".

And one of the most famous lines in the Bible is "Be still, and know that I am God."

Being still really is essential to our wellbeing.

What do we really know of any depth when we are busy? Stuff that has to be done now is generally fleeting stuff, soon replaced by more fleeting stuff.

Shutterstock.

We could live a life like that, but where would be the value in it?

Busyness wraps itself around us, insulates us from the reality of our spiritual journey.

Silence strips that insulation away, giving us a better connection.

I was alone at home when a voice in my head suggested a friend who was thousands of miles away might need help.

Later, she told me that at the same time as I had been hearing that voice, she had been on her knees praying.

I would never have heard that call had I been busy.

As a woman in Biblical times, Mary didn't have the option of walking away from it all as we do, but still, twice, we are told that she found the time to ponder in her heart the presence and the words of her son. She took the extra time.

When her son grew and began his mission, he regularly took time apart from the crowd to listen to what his father had to say.

Time set apart is essential if we want to be in this world, but not completely of it.

The thoughts we don't normally think won't arrive while we do what everyone else is doing.

Perhaps that's why we so often need to be encouraged to slow down, to step away.

But there is no denying it's all for the good.

So perhaps we might approach it gently.

Perhaps with a cup of tea when the rest of the family are still asleep, or with a friend we feel comfortable enough to be silent with.

Be still in a way that works for you, and experience the good of it for yourself.

Don't wait for a transatlantic storm to make it happen.

Oh, and we got the money for the suite back. Thank goodness! ∎

A Year In Nature:
Winter

Fascinating facts about
Mountain Hares

■ Scotland's native hare, the mountain hare, was thought to have moved to the Highlands after the brown hare took over the Lowlands. It doesn't burrow into the tussocky, rocky mountains, but creates small, sheltered depressions called forms.

■ They're at their most distinctive in winter when their characteristic white fur comes in. They blend in with the vegetation poking through the snow.

■ Although hares prefer to avoid predators by running across the hillside in a zigzag pattern, they can clock an impressive 40 miles per hour when given the opportunity to run in a straight line.

■ Living in Scotland's mountains, they can handle winds over 100 mph, temperatures down to -30°C and deep snow. Broad feet help them pad over heavy drifts, and dense fur and squat bodies help them handle the cold and the wind chill.

■ A university study found that hares aren't adapting to climate change, in that they still turn white and stay white until April, despite decreasing snow cover. Other species, like Arctic foxes, have adapted to reduced snow seasons, but it's thought the hares aren't in a rush to change as there aren't as many predators hunting them.

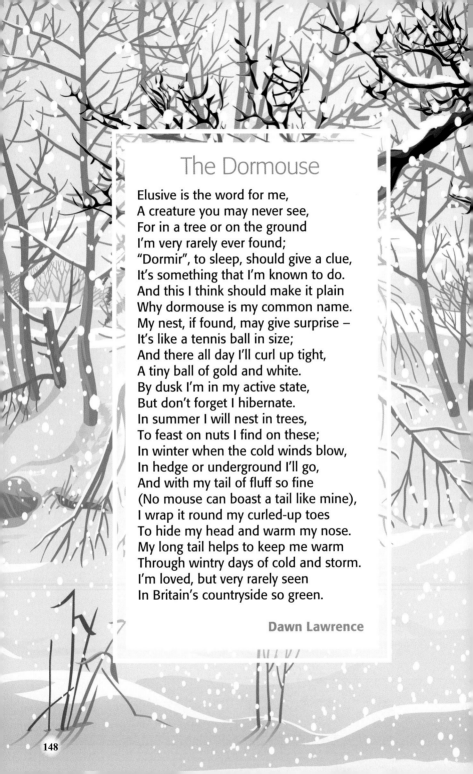

The Dormouse

Elusive is the word for me,
A creature you may never see,
For in a tree or on the ground
I'm very rarely ever found;
"Dormir", to sleep, should give a clue,
It's something that I'm known to do.
And this I think should make it plain
Why dormouse is my common name.
My nest, if found, may give surprise –
It's like a tennis ball in size;
And there all day I'll curl up tight,
A tiny ball of gold and white.
By dusk I'm in my active state,
But don't forget I hibernate.
In summer I will nest in trees,
To feast on nuts I find on these;
In winter when the cold winds blow,
In hedge or underground I'll go,
And with my tail of fluff so fine
(No mouse can boast a tail like mine),
I wrap it round my curled-up toes
To hide my head and warm my nose.
My long tail helps to keep me warm
Through wintry days of cold and storm.
I'm loved, but very rarely seen
In Britain's countryside so green.

Dawn Lawrence

Do You Have A Dream?

Do you have a dream?
Do you keep it in a box?
Or at the bottom of a chest of drawers
Underneath some socks?
Is it hiding in your wardrobe?
Or down below the stairs?
Do you never tell a soul
Because you think that no-one cares?
Is it sealed up in the attic?
Or in a biscuit tin?
Did you shove it in a plastic bag
Then put it in the bin?
Perhaps you sewed it in a cushion?
Or locked it in your heart?
Or marked it "To do later"
'Cause you didn't know where to start?
Is it hidden up the chimney?
Or buried beneath a tree?
Well, only you know where it is,
So go and set it free!

Dave Dutton

The Cathedral Spire

It was faith and dedication
That built this spire so high;
An ecclesiastical compass point
Directed at the sky.
And when it was constructed
Nothing stood in heaven's way,
Except, at night, the moon and stars
And the sun, alone, by day.

It could not be imagined,
As the centuries all passed by,
How there would be so many things
Now filling up that sky.
Helicopters, planes and drones,
Countless satellites,
Rockets launched to outer space,
Seeking further heights.

Yet resolutely it remains,
Solid, firm and true,
Leading our eyes upwards,
To that constant point of view.
Though much in modern life is good
We never must lose sight
Of what there is above us all:
The way, the truth, the light.

John Darley

153

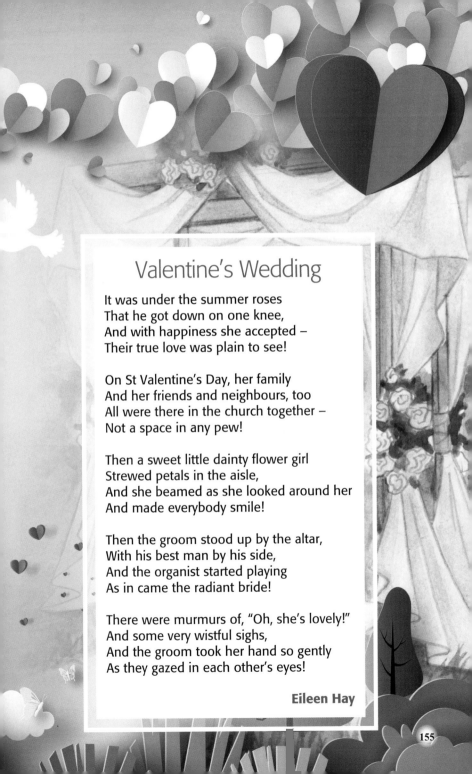

Valentine's Wedding

It was under the summer roses
That he got down on one knee,
And with happiness she accepted –
Their true love was plain to see!

On St Valentine's Day, her family
And her friends and neighbours, too
All were there in the church together –
Not a space in any pew!

Then a sweet little dainty flower girl
Strewed petals in the aisle,
And she beamed as she looked around her
And made everybody smile!

Then the groom stood up by the altar,
With his best man by his side,
And the organist started playing
As in came the radiant bride!

There were murmurs of, "Oh, she's lovely!"
And some very wistful sighs,
And the groom took her hand so gently
As they gazed in each other's eyes!

Eileen Hay

After The Snow

The snow in the town
Has softened the scene,
Made everything equal,
Everything clean.
But as traffic begins
And footsteps appear
This pure, pristine image
Is no longer clear.

But the snow on the Downs
Is like sugar, refined,
And, as the sun rises,
Things are clearly defined.
And only my prints
And some birds, badgers, too,
Are all that disturbs
This beautiful view.

At times winter seems
Like one endless night
But when the snow falls
It makes everywhere bright.

John Darley

157

Blessed Are The Dressmakers

I'm looking through an album
Of photos from the past,
My family in sepia,
Snapped moments that now last.
The dresses take my breath away:
Sleeve ruffles, bias lines,
And '50s silken bridesmaid gowns
Like "Vogue" from past chic times.
There are brides with veils of lovely lace,
No doubt all sewn by hand,
Which brings me to the thing that stalls me
Like a touching hand.
My grandma made these precious clothes;
She trained with patient care,
And each, a handmade masterpiece,
Transports me right back there.
I feel so very lucky
To see how much she blessed
The wearers of these garments
That could sit among the best.

Judy Jarvie

Keeping Busy!

How to keep on being cheerful
When one is often not,
I thought was quite impossible,
Except that I forgot
That when my mind is active,
And I am busy, too,
Time flies by so quickly
Whatever task I do.

I sing myself a happy tune,
The liveliest I know,
And soon my work is finished,
Although I might be slow;
So when trouble visits unannounced
And knocks upon my door,
I don't get all frustrated
And downhearted any more.

I turn my back the other way,
I turn another page,
And trouble leaves quite quickly
When I tell him, "I'm engaged!"

Dawn Lawrence

from the Manse Window

An Olive Branch

AS the season of winter begins, even as early as the end of October, Christmas will already be on the minds of shopkeepers and traders.

Once Bonfire Night has passed, at the beginning of November, shelves will be cleared, stock overhauled, and the usual display of glittering Christmas merchandise will appear in all its glory.

I remember many years ago, as a card trader with a stall at a county show, putting my foot down about selling Christmas cards in August, only to find that the charity stalls nearby had sold out of their entire range of Christmas packs.

"People like to get organised early on," I was informed.

In these difficult days of ever-soaring prices, I can now appreciate the need for many to spread the costs of the Christmas season over a few months.

The variety of Christmas cards on display says a lot about what Christmas means for many today.

There seem to be more koala bears, hares and hedgehogs than donkeys, more pictures of snowy landscapes than scenes of Bethlehem, and even the depictions of Bethlehem and the wise men look as though they have all the wealth of Dubai!

But one design we can be sure of seeing every year is a dove, often with an olive leaf or small twig in its mouth.

The dove is usually a striking white, sometimes speckled with gold, the night sky behind it either an inky blue or a deep red. There is often a star shining brightly overhead and sometimes the word "Peace" is inscribed.

Have you ever wondered what a dove and an olive leaf have to do with Christmas?

The dove bearing an olive leaf comes from the old story of Noah and the flood found in the book of Genesis.

Although usually told as a colourful, fun story of all sorts of animals marching two by two into an ark that God had told Noah to build, the reason for ▶

iStock.

By Janice Ross.

162

the command was actually because God was extremely angry at the great wickedness on the earth.

Genesis chapter six must be one of the saddest chapters in the whole Bible. It tells us that such was the evil in mens' hearts that God was grieved and his heart was filled with pain. He decided to wipe out all his creation except for one man, Noah, and his family, who had stood out as God-fearing and righteous.

And so the waters flooded the earth for 150 days.

Imagine Noah's little family enclosed in the ark for all that time. What was happening outside? How much longer would they be holed up in this dark and smelly place? What would they find when God opened the door – if God opened the door?

When the rain finally stopped and the waters began to recede, Noah sent out a raven.

This bird didn't return, probably because it found dead carcasses to gorge on.

Then he sent a dove. On its first flight this little bird found no resting place and it returned to the ark.

But seven days later it was released again. This time the dove returned, a fresh olive leaf in its mouth, showing that the lower altitudes where olives grew were now above water. God had begun to renew plant life on earth.

The terrible season of God's judgement was over. Ever since that day, a dove with an olive leaf has been a symbol of peace and deliverance.

We may still be wondering what this has to do with Christmas. Well, sadly, Noah and his family were not perfect, and before long they, too, committed sins.

But God remembered his promise never to wipe out man again, never to send a flood to cover the whole earth.

This time, to solve the problem, he sent a baby – like the dove, small and delicate but resilient.

This baby was to be called Jesus, because he would save his people from their sins; he was to be called Immanuel, meaning "God with us"; and he was to be called the Prince of Peace, because only by accepting the sacrifice of his death in our place could we ever have peace with God.

When he grew up, God's only son would present his own life as a sacrifice for the sins of the whole world.

Canterbury Cathedral has stained glass illustrating the presentation of Jesus as a newborn at the temple. It shows the high priest, Mary holding Jesus, and Joseph standing to the side with a basket of a pair of turtledoves, a sacrifice offering to God.

Again we see a dove present when Jesus is baptised in the River Jordan.

As Jesus is commended by the voice of his Father, the dove flies down and lands on his shoulder. John the Baptist recognised this as a sign that Jesus was indeed the promised, long-awaited Messiah of Israel. Love and peace and deliverance had come to us.

It may well be that at some point in our lives we will be called upon to "extend an olive branch".

This idiom, meaning to settle a dispute or resolve an issue, is now widely used.

It might be something as simple as picking up the phone when, really, it should be the other person who does it. Or backing down in an argument over a decision at work, when you know you are right.

It might take a great deal of courage and humility to take this action, as it often suggests that you are admitting your wrongdoing and regret.

So a card showing a dove with an olive branch is a very meaningful Christmas message. It symbolises exactly what Jesus did.

He had wronged no-one, but he would willingly decide to accept all our wrongdoing so that we might go free. Through him we have peace with God.

May you know his peace this Christmas season.

A Year In Nature:
Winter

Fascinating facts about
Owls

■ Owls cannot turn their heads a full 360 degrees, though they can manage up to 270 degrees each way. They need to rotate so far as their eyes can only see about 70 degrees of vision together (binocular vision). Humans see 140 degrees with both eyes.

■ Their night vision is second to none, with five times as many light-sensitive cells on their retina as us. Those eyes are also proportionally very large, not far off the size of ours for an animal so much smaller.

■ Barn owls are the most common land bird in the world. They exist on every continent except Antarctica! Naturally, you won't find many in Saharan Africa, but they're also absent from most of Canada and large swathes of central and northern Asia.

■ Eastern Asia is home to Blakiston's fish owl – the largest owl on the planet with an enormous wingspan of up to 6 feet 3 inches. To stay safe, this huge bird nests at least 12 metres off the ground.

■ With hearing as good as a cat's and super-soft feathers that allow them to glide almost silently, they're effective hunters. In fact, their hearing is crucial to their hunting skills, allowing them to pinpoint the distance, height and direction of any sound from their prey.

Circle Of Gold

I feel I am surrounded by a circle of gold
Made up of true friends, some new and some old,
Some there for me whatever, whenever, for ever,
Not just in sunshine, but for all kinds of weather.

When I need someone to talk to, I never despair;
I know I can call and I know I can share.
There is so much love in this little fold
And they feel the same — or so I've been told.

Tina Cathleen MacNaughton

A Walk In The Park

I didn't want to go for a walk in the park;
I was running on empty, I had lost my spark.
Deep, crunchy frost covered the grass,
The lake now a frozen mirror of glass,
Squirrels and robins darted amidst the trees,
Children made a slide, pretending to be on skis,
Dogs chased sticks, gambolling, having fun,
Frost shone like diamonds in the weak wintry sun.
Although branches were bare, I heard whispers of
    spring –
I had refilled my tank; I could hear my heart sing.

Sharon Haston

171

Journeys

It's from this place the lane and stream
Both their journeys start,
Separated by a hedge,
Which keeps each one apart.

The lane may carry hikers,
Or a rider on a horse,
Whilst the stream keeps calmly flowing
As it spills out from its source.

But further on they'll widen,
Changing subtly, day by day,
Till the stream becomes a river
And the lane a motorway.

And so it is with people
As we journey and we grow,
Discovering a broader view
From what we used to know.

Our horizons may spread further,
Our ambitions drive us on,
But it all begins with something small
For us to set upon.

John Darley

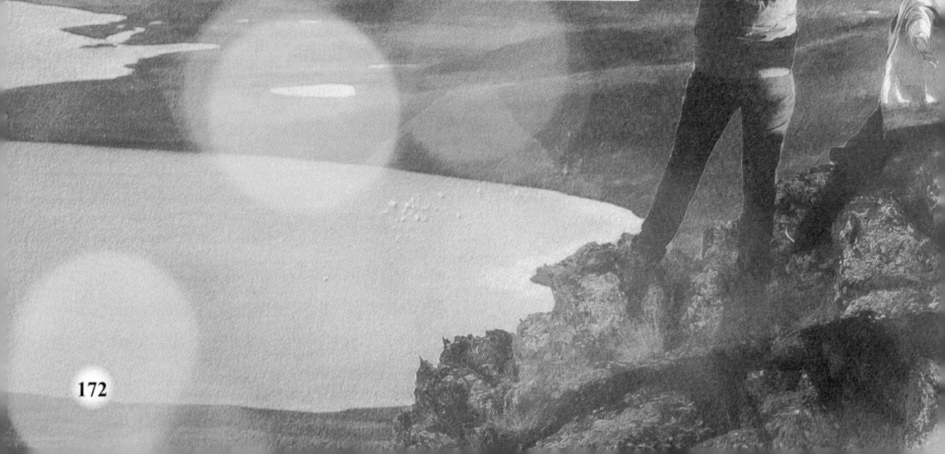

Try to be a rainbow in someone's cloud.

– *Maya Angelou*